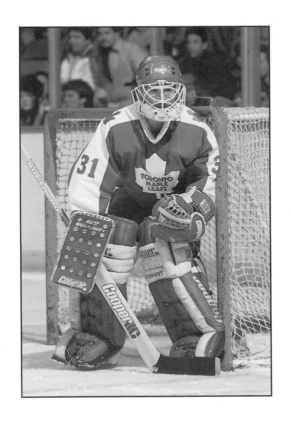

Ed Olczyk

MAPLE LEAFS

TORONTO

BY ROSS RENNIE

CREATIVE EDUCATION INC.

Dedicated to Andrew Pearson

Published by Creative Education, Inc.
123 S. Broad Street, Mankato, Minnesota 56001

Designed by Rita Marshall
Photos by Bruce Bennett Studios,
Frank Howard/Protography and Wide World Photos

Library of Congress Cataloging-in-Publication Data

Rennie, Ross.
   The Toronto Maple Leafs/by Ross Rennie.
   p.   cm.
   Summary: Presents, in text and illustrations, the history of
the Toronto Maple Leafs hockey team.
   ISBN 0-88682-290-4
   1. Toronto Maple Leafs (Hockey team)—History—Juvenile literature.
[1. Toronto Maple Leafs (Hockey team)—History.   2. Hockey—History.]
I. Title.
GV848.T6R46   1989
796.96'264'09713541—dc20   89-37739
                                                            CIP
                                                            AC

THE BEGINNINGS: 1917–1945

During the 1600s and 1700s, Indians used the land connecting Lake Ontario and Lake Huron as an overland route, vital to their existence. Later, this site was chosen to be the capital of the Canadian province we now know as Ontario. In 1834 this settlement was renamed Toronto, the Huron Indian's word for "meeting place."

Today Toronto is the chief communications, manufacturing and financial center of Canada. It has the largest metropolitan area population in the nation and is one of Canada's busiest ports on the Great Lakes. The city is also a major cultural center, with a large system of museums

Turk Broda, shown in action during a 1936 contest, was Toronto's greatest goaltender.

and libraries. Truly, Toronto has more than lived up to its name.

In the world of sports, the city has long served as a meeting place for generations of hockey fans who have followed the trials and triumphs of the Toronto Maple Leafs.

1 9 1 7

Toronto joined the NHL during the league's inaugural season.

The story of the Toronto Maple Leafs, who were first organized in 1917, is largely the story of Conn Smythe. A Toronto native, Smythe was a World War I flying ace. He returned home a national hero and began a career in hockey. He coached several teams, including the University of Toronto team that won the Allan Cup for the senior championship of Canada in 1926.

After acquiring a sizeable sum of money, Smythe decided to fulfill his lifelong ambition of owning a professional hockey team. Backed by sports-minded friends, he organized a group that bought the St. Patricks for $165,000. He promptly changed the club's name to the Maple Leafs.

Although the Great Depression was in progress, Smythe ordered the construction of a new arena for his team. Despite the economic crisis, Maple Leaf Gardens was usually filled to capacity because Smythe stocked his team with young stars such as Frank "King" Clancy, Harvey "Busher" Jackson, Joe Primeau, and Charlie Conacher.

The Leafs won the Stanley Cup in 1931–32 and continued to thrill National Hockey League audiences with their flamboyant style until the outbreak of World War II, when Smythe once again joined the armed forces. In 1942, ten years after their first Stanley Cup, the Leafs captured the Cup once again. Coached by Clarence "Hap" Day, they

As in the 1930s, the Leafs of the 1980s were loaded with young talent like Allan Bester.

Howie Meeker recovered from a war injury to play right wing for the Leafs.

defeated the Red Wings in a seven-game Stanley Cup final, regarded as one of the most thrilling in hockey history.

The Leafs did in that series what no other team had ever done before. They came back to win four straight games after being down three games to none. While Smythe was still in Europe, the Leafs again won the Cup in 1945. Upon Smythe's return, however, the Leafs were floundering at the bottom of the NHL and Smythe decided to rebuild the club with youth in that first season following World War II.

A DYNASTY EMERGES: 1946–1968

The rebuilding of the Toronto Franchise affected the entire team.

Turk Broda returned from the army to play goal. In front of him on defense were two juniors recruited from St. Michael's College, Jim Thomson and Gus Mortson, later known as the "Gold Dust Twins."

Howie Meeker, whom doctors said would never play again due to an injury from a hand grenade while overseas, was on right wing with Ted Kennedy and rookie Vic Lynn.

At the beginning of the 1946–'47 season, Smythe felt his team was at least two years away from another Stanley Cup. When the Leafs actually did win the Cup that season, Smythe was as surprised as anyone, but now he sensed greatness.

The Leafs started the 1947–'48 season coached by Hap Day and were struggling into the beginning of November. Smythe knew this team had a chance to be one for the ages, but there was one missing ingredient. On November 3, 1947, Smythe completed one of the biggest deals in hockey history, trading five players to acquire Max Bentley. The team gave up the complete high-scoring forward line of Stewart, Bodnar, and Poile, as well as defensemen Goldham and Ernie Dickens, for the offensive superstar.

"I made a big gamble," Smythe explained at the time, "but I think it's worth it. I got the league-leading scorer for center-ice duties." The deal rocked the hockey world. Now more than ever, the Leafs became the marked men of the league. Their opponents set out to defeat them any way possible—if not with skill, then by brawn. Hardly a game was played in which they weren't involved in a brawl. This inspired Smythe's famous comment "If we can't beat 'em in the alley, we can't beat 'em on ice."

The Leafs slowly began climbing higher in the standings. By December, Max Bentley had helped propel the team into sole possession of first place. But they were being challenged by their bitter rivals, the Detroit Red Wings. The teams hated each other so much that in a December melee involving all the skaters on the ice, even the goalies fought.

So powerful had the Leafs become that sooner or later every club in the league registered a protest against them. But the Leafs' greatest power to infuriate was in their scoring ability. They so enraged Montreal coach Dick Irvin with a 3–0 win at Montreal on December 26 that Irvin kicked a Santa Claus out of the Canadiens' dressing room after the game

Despite all the charges and accusations against the Leafs, especially "Wild" Bill Ezinicki, who on two separate occasions was charged with deliberately injuring Red Wings goalie Harry Lumley and knocking New York Ranger Edgar Laprade unconscious, the team really had some

1 9 4 7

Bill Ezinicki's aggressive defensive play earned him notoriety throughout the league.

Gary Leeman's play in the 1980s showed hints of Max Bentley's genius.

Borje Salming was Bill Ezinicki's modern-day counterpart.   11

Center Tod Sloan was a standout performer on the Leafs' championship squad.

characters. One was Johnny "Goose" McCormack, perhaps the funniest of them all. He was brought up from the Toronto Marlboro farm club, but was eventually bounced by Smythe because he got married in midseason. Smythe felt that was enough to distract him from his obligations on ice.

Known for his colorful past, Smythe insisted he had mellowed. Yet Smythe battled wherever he and the Leafs went. But he also promoted temperance. He neither smoke nor drank and had little patience with those who did. He twice introduced the team's captain to a national radio audience as "Syl Apps, our captain who does not smoke or drink."

But even the soft-spoken and reserved Apps became infected with the Leafs' battle spirit. He fought with Ralph Nattrass, a tough Chicago defenseman, in a February game, threw him down and pinned him to the ice. He received as much acclaim from the 13,000 fans as if he had scored an important goal.

Apps received headlines again when he announced he would retire at the end of the season, although he was in the prime of his career. But this announcement was overshadowed by the championship race.

Going into the final weekend of the season, the Leafs had a one-point lead over Detroit, with the teams scheduled to face each other in one last home-and-home series. If the Leafs won, they'd have the championship. But more than just first place was at stake. Goalies Turk Broda and Harry Lumley were tied for the Vezina Trophy, and the soon-to-retire Apps needed only two more goals to reach the two-hundred-goal mark.

Turk Broda won the Vezina Trophy for allowing the fewest goals throughout the season.

The weekend concluded in Hollywood-script fashion. The Leafs won both games by scores of 5–3 at home and 5–2 in Detroit, Turk Broda won the Vezina, and Apps scored a hat trick in Detroit to reach and surpass the 200-goal mark.

The Toronto players found themselves matched against their nemesis, Detroit, in the Stanley Cup finals. But the Leafs had little trouble with the Red Wings this time. There was no question about who were the champs as the Leafs routed the Red Wings 7-2 in the fourth game to sweep the series. When it was over, Smythe recalled his preseason comment: "This is the greatest team I've ever had."

After losing the championship to Detroit the following season, the Leafs rebounded to win the sacred Stanley Cup in the 1950–51 season. But at that point the dynasty came to a sudden end.

Toronto lost defenseman Bill Barilko in a plane crash.

This tragedy seemed to trigger a period of decline for the Maple Leafs. Not until 1958–59 did Toronto again make it into the Stanley Cup finals. By then The Leafs' front office realized it was time for a shake-up.

Toronto invited George "Punch" Imlach, player and personnel director for the Bruins, to join the Leafs' organization. Punch's first move as general manager was to fire coach Billy Reay. Imlach looked around for the best possible successor until he realized that he was the man most likely to succeed. He began to rebuild the team. Punch first made the somewhat unlikely acquisition of thirty-three-year-old goalie Johnny Bower, a New York Rangers' reject who had been playing with Cleveland of the American Hockey League.

During the 1958–59 season, Toronto played sluggish hockey and were in last place until the end of the season. They finished by winning five games in a row and made the play-offs on the final night of the season. In a remarkable comeback, Toronto then battled to the Stanley Cup finals before bowing to Montreal.

Toronto now had the makings of a very strong team. Johnny Bower was in goal; in front of him were defensemen Marcel Pronovost, Tim Horton, and Carl Brewer; the forwards were Frank Mahovlich, George Armstrong, and Bob Pulford. They made up the nucleus of the team that returned the Stanley Cup to Toronto for three consecutive years starting in 1961–62.

Perhaps the best of these players was Frank Mahovlich. Mahovlich was one of the finest rookies the Leafs had ever known. He won the Calder trophy in the 1957–58 season and was one of the major reasons for Toronto's championship success. He amassed over a thousand points during a

NHL career which spanned nearly two decades and included six Stanley Cup victories.

Despite the gifted
Frank Mahovlich
and Ron Ellis (Page
17), Punch Imlach
always looked for
more talent.

Despite the presence of Mahovlich and other gifted players on his team, Imlach was never satisfied with the talent on his squad.

On February 22, 1964, Imlach traded five players to the New York Rangers for Andy Bathgate and Don McKenney. These two players combined for twenty-one points for their new club during the play-offs and propelled Toronto to their third consecutive Stanley Cup.

The Maple Leafs again captured the NHL championship

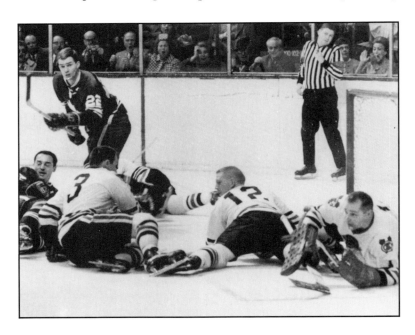

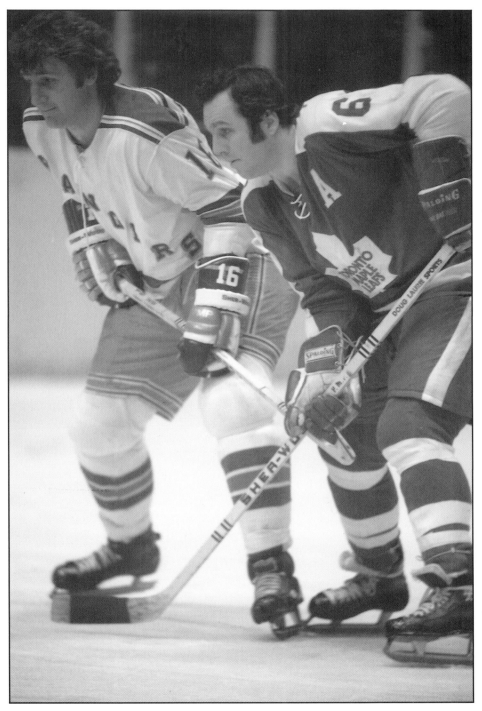

Paul Henderson's career spanned the 1960s and '70s.

Throughout his career, goaltender Jacques Plante allowed only 2.37 goals per game.

in 1967 despite having a squad with an average age of over thirty years. But trying times were just ahead for the Leafs. During two of the next three seasons, they failed to even qualify for the play-offs. Finally, the Leafs realized that Punch could be blamed for some of the team's problems. Although he had guided his charges to four Stanley Cups in ten years of coaching and had got them in the play-offs every year but one, Punch's time had passed.

A NEW ERA BEGINS: 1969–1979

A reorganization took place in 1969–70 as Jim Gregory was named the new general manager and John McLellan took over the coaching duties. The two inherited a spirited young team that didn't win very often but showed promise. The additions of veterans Bob Baun and George

Armstrong brought maturity and balance to the club. Their leadership was evident from the very beginninng.

The first thing Baun did when he arrived in the city was invite the entire defensive squad to lunch. They sat for hours and discussed the game. They came out unified and dedicated to each other and to the purpose of winning.

As Baun explained, "What we're trying to work out is a consistent system of working together. Along these lines, I think, it's worthwhile to have somebody act as the leader."

Armstrong's experience was also beneficial to the club. The "Chief," so nicknamed because of his Indian background, had retired roughly once a year for the past few seasons. He had not bothered to make training camp in 1970, figuring he was not worth it to the club. But when he watched the Leafs struggle in each game, he realized he could help. "It was murder sitting in the press box when I felt I could be helping on the ice," said Armstrong.

The Leafs also needed help in the nets. Goaltender Bruce Gamble was playing well, but couldn't get the rest he required in order to play consistently. So Gregory obtained veteran Jacques Plante from St. Louis. Plante was nearing the end of his eighteen years in the NHL, but still was effective. Throughout the course of his career Plante played with five different teams and appeared in over eight hundred games. He allowed a mere 2.37 goals per game.

When the Chief returned, the Leafs started on their way. Suddenly, one was reminded of the team of aged veterans that had carried Toronto to a Stanley Cup victory in 1966–67. The team once again was putting its faith in old-timers. Plante was forty-two, Armstrong almost that, and Baun was a supposedly washed-up thirty-four. The Leafs hoped that

1 9 7 0

The acquisition of veteran Bob Baun brought maturity and direction to the club.

Bob Baun's leadership was evident during Toronto's 1967 championship season.

these veterans would help return the club to greatness.

Dave Keon was also doing his share to spark the club. The small center was having his best season. For some reason he was playing with more confidence. "It's not that I'm doing things this year I wasn't doing before, but I'm doing them better," he explained.

Old "Jake the Snake" Plante was enjoying success as well. The goaltender had already won the Vezina Trophy seven times and began to vie for number eight as the Leafs came to life. Said the graying goaltender, "I know it's incredible, almost unbelievable, but I'm playing better now than when I was with the Montreal Canadiens. My reflexes are just as fast, and I have a far greater knowledge."

1 9 7 1

Veteran goaltender Jacques Plante enjoyed renewed success with the Maple Leafs.

When the morale on a team is as good as it was on the Leafs, only good things can happen. And they certainly did. In early December, the Leafs embarked on a 15-3-2 rampage. Their thirty-two points in twenty games brought Toronto from last place to within three points of Montreal in third place.

Even coach John McLellan was encouraged as the 1970–71 season moved toward the halfway point. "We started off at absolute rock bottom," McLellan said, "then the guys started to come on. I can't give them enough credit."

To strengthen the club Mike Walton, goaltender Bruce Gamble, and a draft pick were sent to the Philadelphia Flyers in exchange for goalie Bernie Parent and another draft pick. Parent was ecstatic about coming to play with Plante, his boyhood idol. Bernie had a great respect for The Old Master.

"When Ernie Wakely went to St. Louis," Parent remarked, "He was just another goalkeeper. After working

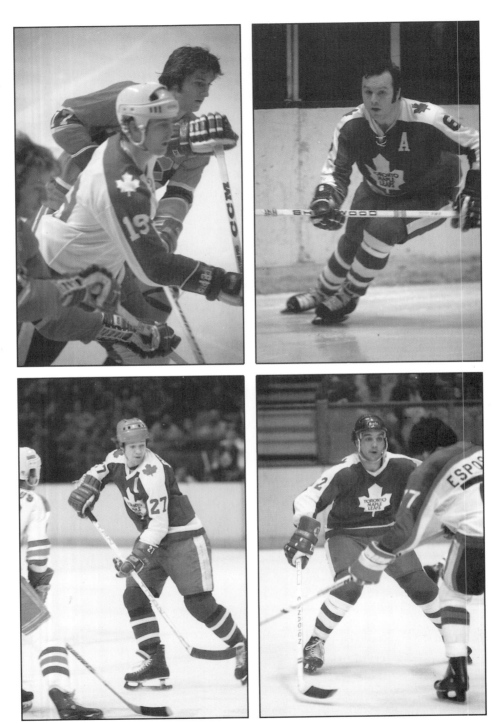

24 *(clockwise): Paul Henderson, Ron Ellis, Dave Williams, Darryl Sittler.*

with Plante for a season, he became a West All-Star. So you better believe I'll take every bit of advice Plante gives me."

The Leafs now had two of the best goaltenders in the game, an organized and controlled defense, and high scoring forwards. The Leafs had the play-off spirit again.

An example of that spirit was the dedication of Bobby Baun. After departing Maple Leaf Gardens after Toronto's 8-1 victory over the Los Angeles Kings on February 13, he got caught in a blizzard on his way home. He had to spend the night at a service station, got home in time to grab an hour's sleep, then snowmobiled part of the way back to the Gardens for a 2:00 p.m. game against the Bruins.

Toronto finished the season solidly in fourth place. The defense, which had made strides under the direction of Plante, Baun, Armstrong and Keon, cut its goals against total from 242 in 1969–70 to 211 in 1970–71. And the Leafs featured three 30-goal scorers: Keon (38), Ullman (34), and Henderson (30).

The only thing hampering Toronto was a series of nagging injuries. But now the season was starting all over again. It had taken the Leafs a long time to get back to the play-offs. Now they were there.

But the final results were less than satisfying. They went up against a solid New York Rangers team in the opening play-off round and lost the best-of-seven series in six games. It was a depressing ending to what was an otherwise promising season, but it was also to set a pattern for things to come. In 1971–72, with Plante and Parent sharing the goaltending, they finished third in the division but were knocked out of the play-offs in the first round once again, this time by the Boston Bruins.

1 9 7 2

The Leafs were eliminated quickly in the play-offs despite the outstanding play of Jim McKenny.

Behind the play of Dave Keon, the Leafs once again qualified for the play-offs in 1972. (pages 26–27)

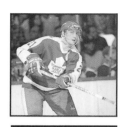

1 9 7 8

Defenseman Borje Salming led the Leafs in assists for the third straight year.

By this time, the World Hockey Association had been born and several Toronto players—notably the fine young goalie Bernie Parent—left the Maple Leafs to play for WHA teams. As a result, Toronto's fortunes declined. The Leafs missed the play-offs in 1972–73 but managed to sneak in the following year only to be wiped out by Boston in four straight games. But better days were coming. In 1974–75 the Leafs finished under .500 and made the play-offs. They knocked off the Los Angeles Kings in the opening round but then were eliminated by a tough Philadelphia Flyers club. Nevertheless, there was cause for optimism. A fine mixture of youth and ability would turn Toronto's hockey fortunes upward in the coming next years.

The Maple Leafs took a serious run at the Stanley Cup in the late 1970s with a roster that seemed to guarantee success. Their goaltender was young Mike Palmateer, whose quick reflexes and combative nature indicated that he would be an ace for several seasons. In addition, the Maple Leafs had superb Swedish defenseman, Borje Salming, and an excellent forward corps. The best of the Toronto attackers were Darryl Sittler, Tiger Williams, and Lanny McDonald.

In 1978 the Maple Leafs scored a major upset, defeating the New York Islanders in a tense and rugged seven-game series. However, the Maple Leafs were thwarted in their run for the Stanley Cup.

TODAY'S TORONTO MAPLE LEAFS:
THE 1980S AND BEYOND

Rick Vaive was the team leader in both goals scored and total points.

The Leafs of the 1980s, guided by club owner Harold Ballard, never realized the potential they exhibited in the late 1970s. Sittler, Williams, McDonald, and Palmateer eventually were unloaded to other clubs. During the decade, the Leafs fought a dismal play-off drought.

The Leafs next made a postseason run for the Cup in April 1986. Once again, the Toronto lineup was sprinkled with gifted youngsters, including goalie Ken Wregget, defensemen Al Iafrate and Gary Nylund, and forwards Steve Thomas, Walt Poddubny, Peter Ihnacak, and Rick Vaive. In addition, Toronto's top choice in the 1985 drift, Wendell Clark had developed into one of the NHL's best rookies.

The Leafs scored a major upset when they defeated the Chicago Blackhawks in three straight games and then extended the St. Louis Blues to a full seven games before bowing to them in St. Louis.

However, in the off-season, Toronto coach Dan Maloney resigned and moved to a similar job with the Winnipeg Jets. He was replaced by John Brophy, who has had considerable experience coaching in the minors. "With the kids we have," said Brophy, "and the way Toronto played in the playoffs, the Leafs should rise again."

But it was not to be. The following season Toronto could only manage thirty-two wins for a total of seventy points. Earning them only a fourth-place showing in the lowly Norris division.

Prior to the 1987–88 season, the Leafs completed a blockbuster trade that sent Rick Vaive, Steve Thomas, and

Al Secord displayed his scoring ability during his first season with Toronto (pages 30–31).

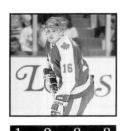

Center Ed Olczyk was Toronto's leading scorer in his first season with the club.

Bob McGill to Chicago in exchange for Ed Olczyk and Al Secord. It was hoped this trade would bring fresh blood and new-found success.

Olczyk, a member of the 1984 US Olympic team, had been the Blackhawks' first choice in the 1984 draft. Although he had a reputation for being a high scorer, he suffered a slump during his last year in Chicago. With Toronto he regained his scoring touch and notched forty-two goals in the 1987–88 season.

Secord, a left-wing, contributed twenty-nine assists during his first year with the club. However, despite making the play-offs, the Leafs were quickly eliminated.

The 1988–89 season was again a tumultuous one for the club. Coach Brophy was replaced by George Armstrong, the team's seventh head coach in the last ten years. Although Armstrong proved popular with the players, the club was troubled by injuries and still struggled. Only the steady play of Olczyk kept the team in the running for postseason play. The end of the year found the club failing to qualify for the play-offs for the fourth time in the decade.

Despite the team's performance in recent years, the Leafs were confident that their fortunes were about to change. With the continued productivity of such players as Olczyk and Secord, combined with a promising group of prospects in their farm system, the Toronto Maple Leafs look forward to improved play in the 1990s and hopefully another shot at the Stanley Cup.